"Whether Rasputin was charlatan or saint remains ambiguous, but *Catastroika* casts the larger-than-life character in new light (or shadow). Told from the perspectives of Rasputin's daughter and a fictional Russian Jew —both settled in America—this book reflects on Russia's past through their experiences. Intimate and insightful, Charles Rammelkamp will have you saying "da!" to *Catastroika*."

    — Eric D. Goodman, author of *Setting the Family Free*,
       Womb: a novel in utero and *Tracks: A Novel in Stories*

"Like Woody   mp's fictional witness to hist   r), was there, and can tell us lu   the assassination of Tsar Alexander I   the Russian revolution, through the murder of the Romanov family. Throw in Maria, Rasputin's daughter and her amazingly picaresque real life in Russia, Europe, and Hollywood, and you've got a tale for the ages. Rammelkamp's diction is pitch perfect for the times he writes about. Read this amazing collection, then read it again."

    — Robert Cooperman, winner of the Colorado Book
       Award for Poetry, for *In the Colorado Gold Fever*
       Mountains

"What a fabulous witches' borscht! It's fabulous in a strict sense: what seems to be the stuff of fable is firmly rooted in the real world. *Catastroika*, a historical novel-in-verse opening with a poem in the author's own voice—his response to viewing a famous part of Rasputin's anatomy in a glass jar in a St. Petersburg museum—moves to a narrative alternating between the voice of Maria, Rasputin's adoring daughter, and that of Sasha, a Russian Jew acquainted third-hand with Rasputin and first-hand with young Maria. Their stories take us from the Romanovs through the Bolshevik revolution to the present day in the US. Meticulously researched, *Catastroika* is peppered with shocks, from the horrors suffered by Jews and "White Russians" in post-Romanov Russia, to the astounding US careers of Maria Rasputin, first as a lion tamer with the Ringling Brothers circus and then—but no, I will commit no spoiler here by revealing her final career. Equally delicious is the later life of Sasha in the US city of —but no, that too would be a spoiler. Suffice it say that *Catastroika*, to borrow a show-biz phrase for a bravura performance, really brings it home."

> — Clarinda Harriss, author of *Innumerable Moons* and other books of poetry and fiction

"Was recent Russian history a matter of *perestroika* (reform), or was it more of a catastrophe? It was a combination of both, as shown in *Catastroika*, a collection of poetic accounts of events that are sometimes ordinary, and other times shattering. The tellers of these deeply felt, often wrenching tales are Maria Rasputin, daughter of the mystic, healer, and ladies' man Grigory Rasputin, and Sasha Federmesser, a Jew who lives through persecution, escapes Russia, and settles in Baltimore. These poems will open your eyes to truths about rulers, revolutionaries, and the people caught between them."

> — Thaddeus Rutkowski, author of *Border Crossings*

"Charles Rammelkamp's *Catastroika* is the best romp with Rasputin since the animated film *Anastasia* – with none of the sugar coating. Based on the true story of Aron Simanovich, Jewish secretary to the notorious monk who perished in Auschwitz, and his friendship with Rasputin's daughter, Maria, *Catastroika* takes us on a thrilling kaleidoscopic ride through some of the most horrific and strangest parts of Russian history."

> — Anne Eakin Moss, professor of Russian literature, Johns Hopkins University

CATASTROIKA

CATASTROIKA

Charles Rammelkamp

Apprentice
House Press
Loyola University Maryland

First Edition

Printed in the United States of America

Paperback ISBN: 978-1-62720-298-5
E-book ISBN: 978-1-62720-300-5

Design by Apprentice House
Editorial development by Annabelle Finagin
Promotion plan by Annabelle Finagin
Cover art by Gene McCormick

Apprentice House Press
Loyola University Maryland
4501 N. Charles Street
Baltimore, MD 21210
410.617.5265
www.apprenticehouse.com
info@apprenticehouse.com

This book is for Abby, the Alexandra to my Nicholas.

The following books were helpful in the
research and formation of this work.

Rasputin: Faith, Power and the Twilight of the Romanovs
by Douglas Smith

Former People: The Final Days of the Russian Aristocracy
by Douglas Smith

Rasputin: The Man Behind the Myth
by Maria Rasputin and Pattie Barham

Jewish Baltimore: A Family Album
by Gilbert Sandler

Contents

Foreword xv
Prologue: Sightseeing in St. Petersburg xvii

SASHA 1
Call Me Sasha 2
Jewels 4
The Decembrists 6
Narodnaya Volya 7
May Laws 9
Sic semper tyrannis 11
Bloody Sunday 13
Kiev Pogrom, 1905 15

MARIA 17
Milochka 18
Strannik 20
Rasputin Goes to St. Petersburg 22
Papa Meets Their Majesties 23
Maria Rasputin Leaves Siberia 24
The Yar Scandal 26
Harry Houdini Gets out of Russia Alive 28
Breaking Up 30
Gossip 32
The Miracle at Spala 34
Rasputin the Healer 36

SASHA 39
The Black Princesses 40
Prophecy 42
Ladies' Man 44
The Prince 46

The Night They Killed Rasputin..48

MARIA **51**
A Cold December Night 52
Identifying the Body 53
Mama..55
Maria Rasputin Marries..56
My Sister Varvara 58
Chain Migration 60
Coincidence 62

SASHA..**63**
Blood 64
Proizvol 65
Byvshie lyudi..66
Protocols 67
Off the Boat 69
One Day in New York...70
The Circus..72

MARIA **75**
Maria Rasputin, Lion Tamer 76
Big Top 78
Exposure 80
The Bear..82
Maria the Riveter 84
Riveting 85
Retirement 87

SASHA..**89**
Operation Former People..90
Yezhovshchina 91
Lev 93
Night of the Murdered Poets 95

The Doctors' Plot 97
Clothes Make the Woman...99
Otkaznik 101

MARIA **103**
The Legend 104
Rasputin's Eyes 106

SASHA.. **109**
Obituary 110
Hitler Is Alive in Argentina 112
Catastroika..114
Rasputin Rehabilitated 115
Saint Petersburg 116
Glossary 119
Acknowledgements...121
Biographical Note 123

Foreword

Grigory Rasputin is an endlessly fascinating character. Apart from his role in Russian history, which has constantly been revised, revisited, reconsidered, the many works of historical analysis in which he figures, Rasputin is a ubiquitous figure in popular culture. The Rasputin character appears in operas, plays, comics, novels, songs and video games: he's everywhere. He's been played by John Belushi in a *Saturday Night Live* sketch, Alan Rickman in an HBO film, Gerard Depardieu in a French-Russian collaboration, *Raspoutine.* He's the villain in 2004's *Hellboy.* He's appeared in an episode of *Buffy the Vampire Slayer* as a demon, and as a sorcerer who sells his soul for power in the Disney animation, *Anastasia.* He's even the title figure in a 1970's disco song, "Rasputin," by the German band, Boney M, a number one hit in Germany and Australia, number 2 in the UK charts. The song has been covered by bands ranging from the Finnish band Turisas as a folk metal song to Boiled in Lead as a folk punk song. A Washington DC band, Ra Ra Rasputin, even takes its name from the song.

There lived a certain man in Russia long ago.
He was big and strong, in his eyes a flaming glow.

The song goes on:

Ra ra Rasputin
Lover of the Russian queen
There was a cat that really was gone

Ra ra Rasputin
Russia's greatest love machine.

Given all this, how could I even begin to find a new angle?
But as it turns out, Rasputin's daughter Maria was no less
fascinating. The only member of the family to escape Russia
after the revolution, she became a cabaret dancer, a lion
tamer in the Ringling Brothers' circus, an American citizen,
a Rosie-the-riveter in the American war effort during the
Second World War. She also wrote several memoirs.

Half the poems in *Catastroika,* which covers more than
a century, are in Maria's voice, and of course her father is
among the many issues she addresses. The other half are
in the voice of Sasha Federmesser, a fictional Russian Jew
who likewise escapes Russia during the turmoil of the early
twentieth century, making his way to Baltimore. Russian
anti-Semitism is another literary and historical theme.

With the United States' complicated relationship with
Russia back in the news, I hope that the historical sketch of
the Russian empire portrayed in *Catastroika* sheds some light
on a fascinating, often troubled culture.

—Charles Rammelkamp
December, 2019

Prologue: Sightseeing in St. Petersburg

The Hermitage? Are you kidding?
The Winter Palace was overwhelming,
but the modest MusEros on Ligovskiy Av.
was the high point.

Sure, we saw the Kolyvan Vase
in the west wing of the Old Hermitage,
largest vase in the world,
like a birdbath for pterodactyls,
after we'd already passed through
the Hall of Twenty Columns,
its amazing mosaic floor,
hundreds of thousands of cubed-tile tesserae;
over three million pieces of art altogether,
largest collection of paintings in the world,
founded by Catherine the Great in 1764, yes,
but the MusEros has Rasputin's footlong dong
preserved in a glass jar,
severed from the mystic when he was murdered
a hundred years ago, in 1916.
They say just seeing it
can cure a man of impotence.

Did it work?
Maybe it was the exotic unfamiliar surroundings,
St. Petersburg so different from Davenport,
or maybe the aphrodisiac qualities of the vodka,

but when we got back to our room at the Pushka Inn,
I hadn't felt such ardor for Alexandra
since the steamy backseat of my parents' car
after football games on crisp Iowa evenings –
my wife's name the same as the Romanov tsarina
rumored to be Rasputin's lover.

SASHA

Call Me Sasha

After the "People's Will," a revolutionary band,
assassinated Alexander II in 1881 –
a bomb tossed in Saint Petersburg –
Jews lost most of the privileges
we'd been granted in Russia.
Alexander, the "tsar liberator," had freed the serfs
twenty years earlier, and we'd benefited as well.

Rasputin originally praised the Black Hundreds,
the nationalist group that promoted Sergei Nilus,
the mystic who later published
The Protocols of the Elders of Zion
as a part of his work on the Antichrist.

But by 1912 he'd mellowed,
defending Jews from our detractors,
calling us "equal before God,"
which made the Black Hundreds turn on him,
mocking him for destroying Orthodox Russia
"for the Yids."

But still, I knew better
than to pursue a friendship
with his daughter Maria,
a lovely fifteen-year-old when I first met her,
fresh to the big city from "The Sleeping Land" –
what "Siberia" means in Tatar, after all;
"The Edge" or "The End" in Ostyak.

"Alexander Federmesser," I introduced myself,
noting my parents had named me for the tsar,
"but you can call me Sasha."

Jewels

Papa knew Rasputin's secretary,
Aaron Simanovich, in Kiev,
where he ran a small jewelry shop –
all Jews knew every other Jew –
but I only became aware of him
when I lived in Saint Petersburg.

Simanovich had brought his son to Rasputin,
suffering from Saint Vitus's Dance,
Ioann, a teenager when the spasms began,
jerking like a puppet,
Pinocchio pulled by strings.

The Petersburg doctors were helpless,
so Simanovich, desperate,
brought Ioann to Rasputin,
who cured him in ten minutes,
laying his healing hands on Ioann's head;
he never suffered from St. Vitus' Dance again.

Simanovich had made a fortune
selling diamonds to the Tsarina's friends,
became Rasputin's secretary, replacing
Ivan Dobrovolsky, who, with his wife,
had been embezzling money
the petitioners brought to Rasputin.

Maria called him by her pet name,
Simochka, fond of the Jew
who'd saved her father when Khvostov,
the Interior Minister, tried to assassinate him.

Later, after the Revolution,
after Felix Yusupov finally did kill Rasputin,
the family moved in with Simanovich,
too dangerous to stay at their father's apartment,
and much later than that,
when Maria'd separated from Boris Solovyov,
she and her two daughters lived with him again,
in Berlin. Her daughters' names?
Tatyana and Maria, after the Tsar's children.

But me? I may have been a landsman,
but I never felt I could approach him.
"Quite a nasty man," the Okhrana reported,
and if you can't believe the secret police,
who *can* you believe?

The Decembrists

It was seventy years before I was even born,
but my uncle told me,
when I was a boy in Kiev,
about the aristocratic officers
who rebelled on Senate Square
in St. Petersburg, in December, 1825,
advocating for a constitution,
the end of serfdom, basic liberties.

The Tsar, Nicholas I, shut it down so fast
it was like dousing a candle in a pail of water.
The leaders were either exiled to Siberia
or executed as traitors,
but they became martyrs
for all future revolutionaries
dreaming of radical change.

As the poet, Prince Alexander Odoevsky, wrote:
Iz iskry vozgoritsa plamya –
"The spark will kindle a flame."
Lenin's magazine, *iskra* – spark –
took its name from the verse.

"Not that it did us much good,"
Uncle Lev added, meaning the Jews,
"but even a little less pressure
of the boot on our necks
is always welcome."

Narodnaya Volya

Papa and Uncle Lev never forgave
"The People's Will" for assassinating Alexander II.
Hailed as Alexander the Liberator,
the Tsar'd liberated the serfs in 1861,
reorganized the judicial system,
promoted university education,
sold Alaska to America.
Life improved even for us Jews.

There'd been three or four attempts on his life already
before Narodnaya Volya succeeded in Saint Petersburg,
March, 1881, that snake, Nikolai Rysakov tossing a bomb
when the bulletproof carriage crossed the Catherine Canal
over the Pevchesky Bridge, the streets flanked
by narrow pavements: the most vulnerable spot.

The bomb killed a Cossack,
but the emperor was unhurt, though shaken.
Still, he left the carriage to inspect the damage.
Another People's Will stooge, Ignacy Hryniewiesky,
hurled another bomb, shouting,
"It is too early to thank God!"

His Majesty's legs shattered, blood pouring,
his feeble cry for help came like a kitten's mew.
Scattered over the snow, bits of clothing,
epaulets, sabers, bloody chunks of human flesh.

Alexander's brutal son, Alexander III, took over,
reversing so many of his father's reforms,
life a greater hardship for Jews especially.
Fourteen years after the assassination,
at my birth in Kiev, over Mama's mild objections,
Papa named me for the Liberator.

May Laws

Talk about a tyrant.
Alexander III really had it in for the Jews,
blaming us for his father's death,
all because a single Jew, Gesya Gelfman,
knew the "People's Will" assassins.

No sooner was Alexander III installed
than his minister of internal affairs,
Nikolai Ignatyev, enacted the May Laws,
restrictions on the freedom of Jews.

We were forbidden from settling
outside the Pale of Settlement,
denied the right to own mortgages,
restricted from having powers of attorney
to manage real property: crippled financially.
Of course, we could not conduct business on Sundays.

Quotas limited the number of Jewish children
admitted to high school or university,
ten percent within the Pale, five outside,
only three percent in Moscow and St. Petersburg,
and then in 1891 all Jews deported from Moscow anyway.

And then there were the pogroms,
more than two hundred
the first two years of the bastard's reign.
The Kiev pogrom of 1881 went on

for three days, my father told me,
leaflets from the workers union stirring them up:
"Do not beat the Jew because he is a Jew
but because he is robbing the people,
sucking the blood of the working man."

Sic semper tyrannis

We spoke Yiddish at home,
but of course we knew Russian,
one of Alexander III's May Laws
mandating the teaching of Russian language
throughout the empire –
Germans, Poles, Swedes as well as Jews.

But when Alexander III died,
the year before I was born,
nephritis, the onset of the kidney failure
attributed to a train accident
six years earlier at Borki,
a village in Ukraine,
when the roof of the dining car
collapsed on the family,
Uncle Lev told me
they all shouted the Latin words
of John Wilkes Booth
when he killed Lincoln, in America.
("Lincoln was a yid, too," Uncle Lev insisted.
"Nu. Just look at him.")

But when Alexander's son and heir Nicholas
heard the news his father was dead,
twenty-six years old at the time,
he broke down crying: "What am I to do?
What is going to happen to me?
I am not prepared to be a tsar.

I have no ambition to be one.

I know nothing of the business of ruling."

Ich kcxk ahf im! Uncle Lev muttered in Yiddish.

I shit on him.

Bloody Sunday

A weakling by any measure,
looking for answers in the oddest places –
occultism, mysticism, fortune-telling and telepathy,
seers and faith healers, prophecies and miracles –
Nicholas brought Russia stumbling
into the unpopular war with Japan
that ended so badly with the humiliation
of the Treaty of Portsmouth in 1905.

Meanwhile worker strikes in cities across the empire
threatened the monarchy, teetering,
fragile as Nicholas' personality.

Troops gunned down hundreds
of demonstrators outside the Winter Palace,
and "Bloody Sunday" lit the fuse
of the Revolution of 1905, a powder keg of protest,
workers walking off their jobs,
the railways brought to a halt,
students protesting in the streets,
mutiny on *The Potemkin* in the Black Sea,
forcing Nicholas to sign the October Manifesto,
granting freedom of speech, assembly, religion,
the formation of political parties.

But in the end, it was no more than a poultice,
a temporary solution.
Uncle Lev called Nicholas a luftmensch,
pushed around by his wife,
building castles in the air.
Bloody revolution now seemed inevitable.

Kiev Pogrom, 1905

The killing and destruction lasted three days,
as many as a hundred Jews killed,
property destroyed – factories, shops, homes.
The historian, Simon Dubnow, called it
Russia's St. Bartholomew's Night.

There'd been a number of bloody pogroms
all across southern Russia
leading up to the horror of Kiev –
Elizabethgrad, Shpola, Ananyiv, others –
monarchists, reactionaries, anti-Semites
proclaiming "all of Russia's troubles stem
from the machinations of Jews and socialists,"
the usual scapegoat story
to bring the blood lust to a boil,
justify the righteous slaughter.

There were those like Prince Zhevakov
who blamed Rasputin: weaving the conspiracy
he was the creation of International Jewry,
part of a plot to destroy Christian Russia.

For me, just about to turn eleven,
both beaten by mobs to bloody pulp and bone,
it was the death of Uncle Lev and Papa
that made up my mind to flee to St. Petersburg.

MARIA

Milochka

This is how my parents met;
this is the story they told me.
A restless young man,
Papa spent his evenings
at a local *kabachok*
drinking vodka and dancing.

Then he met mama at a festival;
they both loved to dance.
They introduced themselves to each other –
Grigori Elimovich Rasputin, Praskovia Federovna
Dubrovina.
"Praskovia Federovna," Papa sighed.
"What a beautiful name, almost
as beautiful as its owner."

Mama blushed, demurred, denied
she was beautiful.

"Ah, milochka," Papa disagreed, calling Mama
his pet name, "my dear,"
as he would all his life;
"You do yourself an injustice."

They became inseparable.
Within a few months Papa announced his intention
to his parents, to marry Praskovia.
Pleased, his father was sure

Praskovia, three years older than Papa,
would cause him to settle down,
lose the foolish mystical ideas he had,
devote himself to family and farming.

Strannik

Papa settled down, built a house
on the family farm
for his growing family,
Praskovia giving birth to four
in rapid succession
though the first, a boy,
only lived a few months,
reminding Papa
of his own brother, Mischa,
making him wonder
if he were being punished
for not obeying the Virgin.

Then even Papa's dreams
like blunt objects beat his head,
dreams of the Virgin of Kazan,
the mother of Jesus,
compelling him to seek his own soul.

Mama feared his restlessness
was her fault, some inadequacy
she couldn't even fathom.
Was she standing in the way
of her husband's fulfillment?

One night she awoke to find him
kneeling before the icon of the Virgin,
his face wet with tears,

and she, too, wept.

"You must do what is right,"
she told Papa.
"There is no time to waste.
If God wants you to find your soul,
you must go."

Rasputin Goes to St. Petersburg

They called it "the Venice of the North" –
Stockholm the rival to that title –
the city Peter the great began in 1703.
Along the banks of the Neva River,
thirty-one islands braided together with bridges,
a monument to God and Russia –
and of course to Pyotr Vyelikie himself.

But when Papa arrived in 1905,
leaving Mama and me in Siberia,
it was also known as "the New Sodom."
Filles de joie filled Nyevski Prospekt,
bordellos brimmed with girls
from Asia, South America, Africa,
brought by the hundreds in ships
sailing into the Gulf of Finland –
French cocottes, Hindu apsareses;
ten-year-old girls in great demand.
Displays of multiple sex partners staged
for appreciative audiences, not to mention
bestial exhibitions of animals and humans.

Commanded in a vision
by the Virgin of Kazan,
Papa had gone to the capital
on a mysterious mission
yet to be disclosed:
not even he knew right away.

Papa Meets Their Majesties

Prince Alexei was a year old
when Papa met the tsar and tsaritsa.
The Grand Duke Nikolasha – known as
"the Evil One" for his temper and cruelty –
he once sliced a pet borzoi right in half
at a dinner party, just to show
his guests how fine his sword was –
brought Papa to the palace in 1905,
but only after the Black Princesses,
Stana, the Evil One's lover, and Militsa,
the two inseparable sisters from Montenegro,
members of the extended Romanov family by marriage,
urged him to, thinking
they could use Papa
to strengthen their position with their majesties.

Of course, this is all just hearsay.
I was what, seven years old at the time,
living in Pokrovskoe with Mama and Varvara.

But Papa was nobody's fool,
more clever than the holy peasant
the Black Princesses took him for.
The empress Alexandra fell under his spell
right from the start.

Or so I heard, anyway.

Maria Rasputin Leaves Siberia

Only a child when my father left the farm
in Pokrovskoe to find his soul,
seeking out holy men and *starets,*
the shock of recognition each time
he returned from his wanderings
was a blast from the Siberian steppes,
that haggard, bearded *strannik*
 with the piercing eyes at our kitchen door.

At ten, my friend Lili invited me
to spend the night with her family.
I was so excited!
But Lili's drunken stepfather started
insisting I kiss him,
slobbering on me, pawing my body.

Horrified, his wife screamed,
"Get your hands off of her, you filthy pig!"
So then he tore off *her* dress,
dragged her to the floor.
Sobbing, humiliated, Lili's mother
tried to shield us,
but her husband continued to maul her
right in front of us.

After he'd fallen into a drunken stupor,
I sneaked away home, shattered.
Our servant Dunia wormed it out of me,

told my father about it;
he was home at the time.
Papa confronted the drunk,
only to be beaten unconscious himself.

So Papa decided then I should leave the village,
its unhappy memories,
accompany him to the capital city, St. Petersburg,
he to continue his mission,
me to begin my life.

The Yar Scandal

Varvara and I were in Saint Petersburg
when Papa took the train to Moscow
that spring I was turning seventeen.
We were mortified
when we heard about the scandal,
all the newspapers full of it.

I swear it was after the Guseva woman
stabbed Papa in the gut in Pokrovskoe in 1914 –
calling Papa a "false prophet, a seducer of honest maidens";
all the newspapers reporting Papa dead,
even the front page of the *New York Times* –
that Papa started to drink again.
He'd given it up as a pilgrim,
but after the stabbing he drank wine
to cope with the lingering pain.

In any case, at the Yar,
the famous Moscow restaurant
where Pushkin, Tolstoy, Chekhov and Gorky
used to go years before,
Papa got stinking drunk,
started grabbing the girls in the Sokolovsky gypsy choir.
He danced like a wildman, they said,
bragged about his relations with the empress,
explicit, obscene,
then pulled out his penis, waved it around,
boasting of his conquests.

The police came, dragged him
cursing and snarling to jail
though he was freed next day
by imperial order,
then headed straight home to Petrograd.

Harry Houdini Gets out of Russia Alive

They said you couldn't escape
from Butyrka, the oldest Moscow prison,
built by Catherine the Great to hold Pugachev,
the Cossack leader of the peasant rebellion.
What great publicity to do so!

Houdini was performing at the Yar,
the dinner theater where Papa, drunk,
had exposed himself a few years before.
His handcuff act was a hit,
but he needed exposure, a sensational stunt.
Years later when I lived in Los Angeles,
stories like this in the showbiz tabloids so familiar!

So the manager of the Yar asked Lebedev,
Moscow police chief, if Harry could attempt
a breakout from the famous fortress-prison.
Lebedev wanted to bring Harry down a peg,
"the man who stumped Houdini."

Stripped bare, Harry was searched up and down,
inside and out – literally –
manacled in heavy iron chains,
shoved inside their Siberian Transport Cell –
the "Carette" they called it – a safe on wheels
used to send prisoners to Siberia.

With a menacing smirk,
Lebedev told him if he failed to escape,
he wouldn't be freed for another three weeks,
not until they got to Sackolin,
where they had a key.

Half an hour later, Harry walked into police headquarters.
But that oaf Lebedev, enraged, refused
to provide the affidavit,
so the newspapers never reported it.

Still, word got around. Houdini's tour was extended.
He even performed for the Grand Duke Aeksandrovich,
the fool who'd be killed by a bomb
a revolutionary tossed into his carriage.

Breaking Up

Iliodor took pride in his celibacy,
a protégé, after all,
of the self-castrating monk, Germogen.
He scolded Papa for his sensuality
like a priggish schoolmarm
admonishing a student who didn't toe the line.

At heart a peasant, Papa lacked tact,
determined to speak truth.
You can take the *muzhik* out of Siberia,
but you can't take Siberia out of the *muzhik*.

So when Iliodor chided Papa for his lustfulness,
Papa reminded him of the time
he visited us in Pokrovskoe,
caught a glimpse of our servant Dunia
while she made her toilette,
her full naked body.
"You know that excited you,"
Papa goaded the monk. "I could tell."

"No!" Iliodor thundered, shocked.
"No! I have *nothing* to confess!
You are lying!
No such thing ever occurred!"

"You know in your heart

I am speaking the truth,"
Papa continued to rile the monk.

"Go! Leave me!" Iliodor fumed.
"You are no friend of mine!
You are a wicked, wicked sinner!"

And just like that,
Iliodor would hound Papa to his grave.

Gossip

It was that anti-Semitic swine, the churchman, Iliodor –
he claimed Russia was "fettered in Jewish chains" –
who slandered Papa, telling stories
of his sybaritic character, like the lie
he raped Prince Alexei's nursemaid, Maria Vishnyakova.

Like a modern-day tell-all gossip
(I haven't lived near Hollywood all these years for nothing),
Iliodor obtained a letter the tsaritsa wrote to Papa,
spread it around so everybody was sure
they were having an affair.

"Come soon," Alexandra had written Papa,
"I am waiting for you
and am miserable without you.
Give me your blessing,
and I kiss your holy hands.
Loving you for all times. Mama."

Even Nicholas saw the letter.
The empress was so incensed,
she had the troublemakers punished,
Iliodor confined to a small, damp room
with iron-barred windows.

Papa denounced Iliodor to their majesties.
"Dear Papa and Mama," he wrote,
"Iliodor's the Devil. An apostate. He's damned."

But you can't un-do gossip, can you?

Later, the swine put the crazy woman Guseva
up to stabbing Papa in Pokrovskoe
that awful day in 1914, all the newspapers
reporting him dead – even the *New York Times*.
Guseva didn't deny her guilt, announced
she did it because Papa was "a false
prophet, slanderer, and a seducer of honest maidens."
Lies that Iliodor'd fed her.

And Iliodor? Shaved his beard, rouged his cheeks,
put on women's clothes, fled to Sweden.
Strange that the man who would succeed him
in killing Papa, Yusupov, was likewise a cross-dresser.

The Miracle at Spala

You've heard of the term "groupie"?
Well, of course you have,
coined in the mid-1960's,
but I'm just an old woman now,
and I never did follow rock stars.
But Alexandra was Papa's groupie,
decades before the word was invented;
he was a god, he could do no wrong.

When, the family was at the villa in Poland
that September in 1912,
eight-year-old Alexei began to complain
about the pains in his legs and abdomen,
Dr. Botkin discovered the hemorrhage in his groin,
but he couldn't do anything to stop the bleeding.
Summoned to Spala from Petersburg,
Doctor Rauchfuss and the imperial surgeon, Fyodorov,
along with Alexie's pediatrician, Ostrogorsky –
all helpless to stop the young boy's misery.

"Mama, please help me! Won't you help me?"
the little boy pleaded; his mother,
distraught at his bedside, wrung her hands,
while Nicholas fled in tears,
unable to watch his son suffer.
The French newspapers reported Alexandra so overwrought,
doctors had to restrain her from throwing herself out a
window.

"When I am dead,"
the little boy asked plaintively,
"it won't hurt any more, will it?"

When newspapers reported the tsarevich near death,
Alexandra looked to Rasputin as her final hope.
Even though the priests had already
administered the last sacrament,
the tsarina telegraphed Papa in Pokrovskoe
to ask him to pray for Alexie.

"God has seen your tears
and heard your prayers,"
Papa replied. "Do not be sad.
The little boy will not die."

The following day the bleeding stopped.

Rasputin the Healer

Papa's reputation as a healer
aroused envy and suspicion,
but grudgingly well-known nevertheless.

There was Olga Lokhtina, a Kazan noblewoman,
who claimed Papa cured her from "neurasthenia of the
intestines,"
from which she'd suffered for five years,
even the Western European specialists
unable to ease her agony, her grief.

There was also Aaron Simanovich, the Jew,
Papa's secretary in Petrograd.
Originally from Kiev, where he'd run
a little jewelry shop, later making a fortune
selling diamonds to the tsaritsa's friends,
Simochka, as I fondly called him, brought his son to Papa,
suffering from Saint Vitus's Dance,
Ioann just bar mitzvah age
when he began jerking like a marionette
yanked by strings.

Rosenbach and Rubinko, the Petersburg doctors,
could do nothing for him,
but when Simanovich, who loved his children
as only a Jewish father can love,
brought him to Papa, in only ten minutes Papa cured him.
After Papa lay his healing hands on Ioann's head,
he never experienced the attacks again.

After Felix Yusupov killed Papa,
Simochka took me and Varvara in.
Later, in Berlin, after I'd separated
from Boris Solovyov,
he took me and the girls in again.
I loved that Jew.

But you know what?
The one he was most famous for –Alexei –
Papa never did "cure" him.
He was a hemophiliac
until the day he died,
killed along with his family
four weeks shy of his fourteenth birthday.

SASHA

The Black Princesses

About the same time as the Kiev pogrom,
precipitating my flight to Saint Petersburg,
Rasputin met Nicholas and Alexandra
for the first time, while having tea
with the Black Princesses,
as Militsa and Stana were called.

Ah, Alexandra! Granddaughter of Queen Victoria,
a German princess from Darmstadt,
she'd have been better off
married to one of the English princes
who proposed to her,
as her grandmother so desperately wanted.
She might have been Queen of England!
But her older sister Elizabeth,
who'd married Alexander III's younger brother
and converted to Orthodoxy, persuaded her
to accept Nicholas' proposal.

"Experts" in mysticism and the occult,
Militsa and Stana, sisters from Montenegro,
part of the extended Romanov clan,
took Alexandra under their dark wings;
Alexandra regarded Militsa as a "prophetess,"
hung like a fly in the web of her words,
convinced for instance when they told her
their older sister Elena, Queen of Italy,
had been "possessed" by an evil spirit.

Alexandra was their dupe, their pawn –
Ferd I can hear Uncle Lev snort, *Yold!* –
just as Nicholas was Alexandra's.

Prophecy

If Catherine the Great's weakness was for lovers –
we all knew the legends of her erotic furniture
in the Gatchina Palace, tables with legs
fashioned as giant penises,
cocks and vulvas carved into cupboards,
statues of a naked man and woman
in her "erotic cabinet" –
it was the mystics and pilgrims –
stranniki – for the Romanovs.

Even before Grishka, there was Philippe,
the charlatan from Paris
who convinced Alexandra she was bearing
a male heir at last,
after the let-down of four daughters,
Anastasia the most recent.
Rumor had it he made her pregnant
via "psychological treatments."

Everyone at court was alarmed,
from the Dowager Empress to Prince Vladimir Meshchersky,
advising Nicholas and his wife
about the danger a man like Philippe posed,
but they wouldn't listen,
even when the head of the tsarist secret police,
Pyotr Rachkovsky, exposed Philippe as phony –
"a dabbler in black magic, a Jew,
a would-be magnetizer."

Only when it became apparent
Alexandra was not with child
did they consent to have Philippe
sent back to France for good
though not before he gave Alexandra
a bouquet of dried flowers
he claimed had been touched by Christ himself.

Alexandra framed those flowers,
kept them in her bedroom,
then moved on to the next mystic
presenting himself as in possession of occult powers,
among them Mitya, the holy fool,
himself replaced by Rasputin.

Ladies' Man

Everybody in Saint Petersburg knew it,
but nobody talked about it,
at least not for a Jew like me to hear,
but Rasputin had a reputation
for hugging and kissing girls and women.

They all fell under his spell,
from Olga Lokhtina, his most ardent believer,
a conventional Petersburg wife, married to an engineer,
to Alexandra herself, the tsarina.

Punished as a horse thief in his youth,
by being tossed in the air, landing on his back,
the punishment caused a mysterious change
in Rasputin's body, rumor had it:
he could keep an erection for as long as he liked,
which won him favor with bored society ladies,
starved for sex. They could not
get enough of him, though Rasputin claimed
he was driving the Devil out of them.
"You demon of the flesh, be gone!"
he screamed as he mounted the women.

"His kisses are chaste and pure,"
his defenders maintained,
and even his wife, Proskovya,
whom he always left behind in Siberia
like a faithful old dog,

never became jealous or angry
when Rasputin groped women in front of her.
At least, that's what I heard.

The Prince

Yusupov? The shlump who killed Rasputin?
A cross-dresser in his youth, a faigeleh.
I didn't know any of this at the time –
how could I, just a Jew in the Tsar's Russia? –
but later I read his memoir, *Lost Splendor.*

An ancient aristocratic family, the Yusupovs
joined the court of Ivan the Terrible
back in the sixteenth century.
They had a standing to uphold.

"A schoolboy by day," Felix wrote,
"by night an elegant woman."
For a time he even sang in a cabaret.
When his family found out,
there was hell to pay.
His *tatteleh* called him a guttersnipe,
made his son take icy morning showers.

Felix tried to take an interest in women,
but he despised courtship,
wanted to be the star,
the one surrounded by admirers.

The whole Yusupov family hated Rasputin,
but Felix sought him out.
Like everybody at the time,
he hungered after spiritualism.

Rasputin's daughter Maria disliked him,
described Felix as "lithe and elegant,
with rather affected manners."
But she never imagined
Yusupov was capable of murder.

The Night They Killed Rasputin

The way I heard it,
Rasputin went to a party
at the Moika Palace, where the Yusupovs lived,
that December night, the end of 1916.

Yusupov offered Rasputin poisoned cakes,
lethal enough to kill a horse,
but apparently they had no effect,
so Yusupov gave him some Madeira,
likewise laced with poison,
but after three glasses, still nothing.

So after a few hours, Yusupov borrowed
Grand Duke Dmitry Pavlovich's revolver,
told Rasputin to look at the crucifix
of rock crystal and silver
standing atop a mahogany cabinet,
and say a prayer.
Then he shot him in the chest.

But even then he didn't die.
"The devil who was dying of poison,
who had a bullet in his heart,"
Yusupov wrote in his memoirs,
fled into the winter night,
followed by Yusupov and the conspirators –
Dmitry, Sukhotin, Lazovert.
They tracked him down like a wounded animal

at the Large Petrovsky Bridge,
tossed him into the icy Neva below,
the body discovered two days later.

MARIA

A Cold December Night

When Papa went out late that night,
I'd a terrible feeling,
but when Protopopov, the Interior Minister,
woke me the next morning with his telephone call,
my dread multiplied a hundred times,
my head almost too heavy to hold up.

"What time is it?"

"Just seven," the Minister apologized,
"but is your father home?"

I checked Papa's room. Empty,
the bed still made, unmussed,
and when I told Protopopov,
all he said was, "Thank you. I must go."

Varvara and I knew,
certain as our own breath,
Papa was dead.

Late that December afternoon,
a police inspector called at the flat,
showed us a bloodstained boot,
which we both recognized as Papa's.
They'd found it on the ice
near the Petrovski Bridge.

Identifying the Body

The day after we saw Papa's shoe,
divers found Papa's body
under the icy Neva.
Protopopov called again with the news.

I'd known in the depth of my soul –
knew and knew and knew –
but Varvara and I'd clung to hope,
a fantasy he'd walk back into the apartment;
now there was no dodging the truth,
a fact huger than my mind could hold.
Stunned, I forgot all about the Minister,
until his voice came over the line again.

"Maria, I hate to do this, but
we need a close relative to identify his body."
Of course I agreed.
"I must warn you, Maria," he added,
"it's not a pleasant sight."

When the car arrived for me,
Varvara insisted on coming along.
They drove us to the Petrovski Bridge,
led us through the deep snow
to a little hut surrounded by officials.

His face smashed in at the temple,
clots of dried blood in his beard,

his right eye dangling against his cheek,
held by a slender thread of flesh.

The horror of recognition on my face
told Protopopov all he needed to know,
but he had to confirm it, police procedure.

"Yes," I gasped, "He is –
he was my father, Grigory Efimovich Rasputin."

Mama

Before we knew the truth,
we'd sent a wire to Mama in Siberia
saying only that Papa was "gravely ill."

It took five days for the train
to reach Petrograd Station from Pokrovskoe.
Varvara and I met them there;
Mama already knew from our appearance,
like a couple of starlings in the black
dresses the tsarina gave us,
Papa was dead.

Mama'd always kept her emotions under control,
but now she broke down,
an ear-piercing shriek, sobbing
as we led her to the car
that would take us back to the flat.

I consoled Mama with a description
of the funeral on the grounds at Tsarskoye Syelo,
the plot donated by Anna Alexandrovna,
his body prepared for burial by Sister Akulina,
but I did not tell her
about the castration, the mutilation of Papa's groin.

Maria Rasputin Marries

Boris wasn't my first love by any means.
I fell hard for the Georgian, Simoniko Pkhakazde,
but Papa objected when we became engaged.
We quarreled. Papa threatened
to send me back to Pokrovskoe
to get me away from my fiancé.

Papa wanted me to marry the son
of his friend from Kazan,
now a bigshot secretary at the Holy Synod.
So Papa tried his hand at matchmaking,
set me up with this Boris Solovyov,
an ensign in the White Army.
Boris had been wounded in the Carpathian Mountains
during the Russian retreat in 1915,
brought back to Petrograd,
unable to return to the war.

Jealous, Pkhakazde planned to kidnap me,
spirit me away to the Caucasus,
even rumored to have attempted suicide.
I broke off the engagement –
Papa was still alive then –
but still I refused to marry Boris.

After Papa was killed, Boris wrote letters
begging me to marry him.
At last I gave in –

it was Papa's wish, after all.

Boris and I married in September, 1917,

Tatiana and Maria coming soon after.

My Sister Varvara

Two years younger than me,
Varvara was like a twin,
close as two fingers twined,
linked by the wonder of our father,
the way the villagers pitied us
for being the spawn of such a strange man,
always wandering off to seek "the truth,"
rumored to be a satyr,
wild orgies with women.

We'd originally gone to the local village school,
but Papa wanted a finer education for us
than Pokrovskoe could offer,
enrolled us in the Steblin-Kamensky School
on Liteiny Prospect in Saint Petersburg,
treated us like princesses.
We shared a room in Papa's apartment on Gorokhovaya
Street,
which was where Papa said goodbye to us,
December 16, 1916. I was eighteen, Varvara sixteen.
"I'm going out, my doves," he soothed,
"Don't be anxious. I've been invited to Prince Yusupov's."
And then he was gone,
the last time we saw him alive.

And Varvara? She didn't escape the Communists
the way I did, separating from Boris
in Vladevostok, then traveling to Berlin

by way of Trieste and Prague,
reuniting with Boris in Paris.

Varvara ended up in Tyumen,
in Siberia, a government stenographer.
"Lord, it's hard," she wrote me,
"my soul is breaking into pieces,
Why was I born?"

She died in Moscow, 1924, typhus,
but I've no doubt the Soviets poisoned her.
She'd been trying to come to me.

Buried in Novodevichy cemetery in Moscow,
her coffin was dug up and discarded
three years later, when then government decided
she wasn't important enough to be buried there.

Chain Migration

I came to the United States in 1935 –
my dream for so many years!
After Boris died in Paris, tuberculosis,
worn out from his jobs
after the restaurant went bust –
all day in the soap factory, night porter, car washer –
just to keep me and the girls fed –
out of the blue I got an offer
to be a cabaret dancer in Bucharest.
My name, not my dancing
got me the job, of course,
but I had taken dance lessons
in the Imperial Theaters in St. Petersburg.

The dances were dreadful
reenactments of Papa's murder.
Every time I was crippled by memory,
often breaking down and weeping,
assaulted by emotion as if with a club.

So in 1929 I joined the circus,
trained as a lion tamer,
traveled throughout Europe for five years,
mindlessly making the animals
circle the ring, audiences amazed
wild animals could be so docile.

Then Ringling Brothers brought me to the United States!

As I say, a dream come true.
The downside? My daughters,
Tatiana and Maria, both teenagers by then,
denied entry by U.S. Customs.

Coincidence

When they met in Greece after World War II,
Irina Yusupova – nicknamed Bébé,
now married to Count Nikolai Sheremetev –
and my younger daughter Maria,
married to Gideon Boissevain,
Dutch ambassador to Cuba
(a very wealthy man),
became fast friends, inseparable,
neither knowing who the other really was.

Russians living abroad after the war,
part of the same social milieu,
they knew better than to probe too deeply.
But still they felt
a natural sympathy for one another,
though too sophisticated
to act like schoolgirls sharing secrets.

Only when they parted did Maria reveal
she was the granddaughter of Grigory Rasputin.
Stunned, Bébé gushed,
"My father killed your grandfather."

SASHA

Blood

After the Romanovs were executed the summer of 1918,
the Reds and the Whites held nothing back,
mutilating one another like something out of the Middle
Ages,
bashing in faces, hacking off heads and limbs,
violating the genitals of men and women,
scalping, burning their enemies alive.
"Red hate and White hate raged side by side
through the beautiful wild country,"
Radzianko, one of the former tsar's men, observed.

And of course, the Jews got it from both sides,
Bolshevik vermin from one point of view,
oppressors of "the People" from the other.

What finally convinced me
I had to get out of Russia wasn't the rumors
of the pogrom in Yekaterinburg, that July, 1919,
a city east of the Urals, over two thousand killed
by the White forces, most of them Jews,
led by the Cossack warlord, Ataman Semenov,
legendary for his savagery.

No, it was the seventeen-year-old boy
hanged in Yalta, solely because his last name,
Bronstein, was the same as Trotsky's.
Who needs a "reason" for killing,
who needs a "reason" for *revenge*?

Proizvol

After Fanya Kaplan shot Lenin in Moscow, the end of 1918
–

a Socialist Revolutionary, she thought him a traitor –
I knew as certain as the cold of a Russian winter
the Jews would somehow be punished.

"The Red Terror is not an empty phrase,"
Fanny's executioner declared,
"There can be no mercy for enemies of the Revolution!"

Sure enough, the bloodlust reached frenzy.
"For the blood of Lenin," one of the party newspapers
shrieked,
"let there be floods of blood of the bourgeoisie –
as much as possible."

Maxim Gorky observed *proizvol* – arbitrary rule –
had become state policy.

The Whites believed bolshevism a Jewish plot,
but the Reds were no less ruthless,
mutilating, raping, murdering in pogroms.
I had to get out.

Byvshie lyudi

I couldn't feel bad for them,
the countesses who now worked as servant girls,
while the servant girls became heads of government offices,
ferried around Moscow in official automobiles.
The aristocrats, untrained to do anything
with any practical value,
sold their furs and silver
in the open-air markets,
just to eke out a living for a few more weeks.

Denied access even to public cafeterias,
the bourgeois pariahs of the Soviet state,
the former people, never identified themselves
as "the son of a count" or "prince,"
just tried to fit in, "pass," slip by,
hidden in the shadows.

Just try being a Jew, I thought.

Protocols

In 1919 Lenin delivered a speech
"On Anti-Jewish Pogroms," on gramophone,
explaining antisemitism in Marxist terms,
as an attempt to divert the hatred
of the workers from the exploiters to the Jews,
linking antisemitism to class struggle.

Ever since Sergei Nilus' bogus book
about the "Antichrist," including
that magnificent forgery, *The Protocols
of the Elders of Zion,* like tossing peat
on the smoldering fire of Jewish hatred,
pogroms had been on the rise across the empire.
Even after Lenin's speech, in March,
the Bolsheviks seized Jewish property
in November that year.
True, the October Revolution of 1917
abolished the Pale of Settlement,
but hatred and suspicion against Jews never ceased.

But by then I was already on my way
to America, and besides, life for Jews
never really improved in the Soviet Union.

How did I escape?
By train from Petrograd to the Crimea,
then into Europe, finally to Baltimore in steerage.
Terrified I'd be discovered on the train,

I thanked my good fortune a boy
named Vladimir Nabokov stole all the attention,
a fop dressed in spats and a derby,
sporting an elegant cane,
a member of the nobility,
likewise on the run
to save his life.
The protocols never change.

Off the Boat

I never thought the streets of America
would be paved with gold;
I only wanted to put distance
between me and the *cheka*.
I had no idea what a "counter-revolutionary" might be,
but I was a Jew and I knew
I would never be safe,
just another insect or rodent to exterminate.

When I got off the boat at Locust Point,
half-starved and sick from the trip in steerage,
I made my way to East Baltimore,
soon had a job in Jacob Epstein's
Baltimore Bargain House, learned to speak English
at the JEA night school on East Baltimore Street,
met my darling Riva at Wartzman's bakery,
settled into my new American life.

I won't say I didn't have nightmares –
pogroms, the *cheka*, gulag labor camps, torture –
but as time spooled out and we were blessed
with Herman, Reuben, Sam and Frieda,
I stopped anticipating the knock on the door,
stopped expecting the door to be kicked in.

One Day in New York

Funny thing, one day in New York, 1922,
where I'd gone with friends from work,
visiting other Jews who'd escaped Russia,
I recognized the woman I remembered seeing
outside the Angleterre Hotel in Petrograd
five years before: Louise Bryant,
I learned was her name.
She'd interviewed the powerful politicians then –
Lenin, Trotsky, Kerensky –
with her husband, John Reed.

Kerensky! He'd come to power in the February Revolution
only to be overthrown by Lenin
in the October Revolution,
his Socialist Revolutionary Party discredited,
which led to Fanny Kaplan shooting Lenin.
But Bryant interviewed him at the height of his power,
when he lived in one of the Romanovs' palaces,
greeted with the ovations reserved for a hero –
only months before
he fled to Paris in disguise.

Now? Reed was dead and Bryant was the main speaker
at a memorial service for him in New York,
here with her new lover, a man named Bullitt,
likewise a journalist, who'd worked for Wilson
at the Paris Peace Conference in 1919
where they wrote the Treaty of Versailles,
created the League of Nations.

"Hey, Sasha, what ya gawking at?"
My pal Iosif shook my shoulder,
knocking me out of my memories.
"Ain't you seen a shikse princess before?"

The Circus

It was the middle of the Depression, yes,
but I still had my job, even though Mister Epstein
sold Baltimore Bargain House, the Butler Brothers
changing its name to American General Corporation.
Riva still worked at the bakery;
people would always need bread.

So we decided to treat the kids
to a show, the circus, Hermie
just about ten, Reuben and Sammy
following two and five years later,
Frieda a babe in arms.

The children kvelled, especially Hermie,
himself the ringmaster in his own circus acts
he staged for us in Druid Hill Park,
making his younger brothers perform –
clown, strongman, acrobat.

Ringling Brothers had bought Barnum and Bailey –
the Greatest Show on Earth –
at the start of the century but they'd only combined
into one grand show around 1919;
running two different circuses too much work
for the last two living Ringlings. Charles and John.

We took the train up to New York,
staying with Riva's brother Isaac's family

on the Lower East Side.

Greeted by a vivid poster,
a woman dancing with a tiger
under the legend,
Intrepid Lady Trainer Wrestling
the Now Friendly Terror of the Jungle,
we took our seats under the big top.

Only after the trapeze artists,
the tumblers, the clowns,
the Giraffe-Neck Woman from Burma,
did the lady lion trainer and her menagerie enter the ring.

I knew I'd seen her before!
Sure she'd died with her father and siblings
during the bloodiest savagery of the civil war,
I hadn't given her a thought in years.

"You look like you've seen a ghost," Riva murmured,
her brows knitting together in concern.

"I think I have."

MARIA

Maria Rasputin, Lion Tamer

I never much liked Boris,
but Daddy told me to "love Boris,"
so a year after Daddy's assassination –
poisoned, shot, bound up,
tossed into the freezing Malaya Nevka River –
we were married, October, 1917.
I was nineteen.

The next decade we lived all over,
Siberia, Ceylon, Suez, Prague,
where we had a restaurant,
Austria, where Maria was born –
she and her older sister Tatiana
both named for the Grand Duchesses;
we might have called another Anastasia, too –
Berlin, where I learned to dance,
and finally Paris, where Boris worked
first in a soap factory, then as a night porter
before he died, tuberculosis, 1926.

Then the fun really began.
I had two children to support.
My first memoir, *The Real Rasputin,*
brought in a little money,
but I was forced to join the circus, a dancer.

After my second memoir, *Rasputin, My Father,*
I got on with Ringling Brothers,

toured America as a lion tamer
until I was mauled by a bear,
had to leave the circus in Miami.

I still remember that reporter
for the Associated Press asking me why
I learned to tame wild animals.

"Why not?" my arch reply.
"I have been in a cage with Bolsheviks."

Big Top

All got up in my beads,
headdress and flowing robe,
looking every bit like Mata Hari,
my wand in hand like a sorceress
to guide the animals around the ring,
graceful with the trained beasts –
even if I wasn't George William Lockhart –
I was still the main attraction
that season at Madison Square Garden.

More popular by far
than the midway freaks –
Miss Alainna Bennett, "Half Girl,"
whose body ended at her hips;
or Miss Dorothy Herbert,
"World's Most Daring Horsewoman,"
Freddy the armless wonder,
Fat Lady Doris Bleu,
Midget Lady, the snake charmer,
the strongman and the trapeze artist
the aerialists with their Hammock Act!
Forget about Chang and Eng,
the original Siamese Twins!

No, *my* poster proclaimed:
Daughter of Imperial Russia's
World-Famous Mad Monk and
Confidant to the Late Czar!

I was a star.

Exposure

With great fame comes great danger.
I admit I often felt vulnerable,
as if the audience were a firing squad;
no telling what crazies might try something –
some Bolshevik exile, some resentful White,
still blaming Papa for the tsar's problems
punishing him by punishing me.

Once I saw a man staring intently,
for all appearances there with his family,
wife, three sons, a baby —
Jews, I was all but certain.
I felt his eyes on me like a pair of Nagant pistols.

Who could they be?
I put my darlings through their paces,
cats and elephants circling the ring,
responsive to the touch of my wand.
But out of the corner of my eye
I watched the man, the Jew, turning pale,
his wife looking concerned.
Maybe he was having a stroke,
but all along I remembered darling Simochka,
our Jewish savior who'd put us up in Berlin,
after we'd escaped Russia.
Poor Simochka would be captured by the Nazis in Paris,
deported to Auschwitz in 1944,
where he was murdered at the age of 72.

But who was this Jew?
Finishing my performance,
I retired to my dressing room, head throbbing.

The Bear

Ever been to Peru?
Little town in Indiana on the Wabash River.
In fact, the Wabash divides the town in two.
The oldtimers call the place "*PEE*-ru,"
though most people say it like the country.
Winter home of the Ringling Brothers Circus,
which was why I found myself there,
the spring of 1935, less than two years
after John Dillinger and his gang
robbed the police department armory,
revolvers, Tommy guns, shotguns, you name it.

My job was animal trainer – lion tamer,
if you want to make it sound glamorous –
teaching these big furry beasts to obey,
follow simple commands.

I had my father's hypnotic eyes,
which may have explained my rapport
with the animals. I played on my name,
Maria Rasputin, you can bet,
to sensationalize my performances.
The advertisements announced me:
"performing magic over wild beasts
just as her father dominated men."

But this bear had other ideas that day,
and I was lucky to escape with my life
after it mauled me, claws and teeth
tearing at my flesh, wrenching my bones.

Only thirty-seven at the time,
I stayed with the circus until we got to Miami,
then I quit, my injuries too severe.

Maria the Riveter

Even after I left the circus,
I stayed on in this country,
marrying Gregory Bernadsky
(later shortened to Bern)
a former White Army officer,
now an electrical engineer,
whom I'd known in Russia,
met again in Miami.

We divorced after five years,
but Gregory was already naturalized,
so I was able to become a citizen, too.
Lived here ever since,
even though Tatiana and Maria
started families of their own in Europe.

During the war? Worked as a riveter,
a machinist in the shipyards,
a job I kept until 1955
when I was forced to retire –
I've often thought because of the Red Scare;
I was naturally suspected of being a Communist
because of my name, Rasputin.
Me! A Communist! After what
those Bolshevik bastards did to me?

Riveting

The high point of my life?
You'll laugh, but it was when I worked
in the shipyards, a riveter during the war.

Not socializing with Russian nobility –
the Tsar's children so sheltered
they were downright boring.
Not the cabaret life in cities across Europe,
those dreadful re-enactments of Papa's murder.
Not the circus life, training wild beasts,
top billing at Madison Square Garden.
Certainly not teaching Russian to the brats
of LA émigrés wanting their children
to know the language, forced
to come to me for lessons.
Definitely not writing books.

But riveting? It was nothing
I ever dreamed of doing,
but once I learned how,
I loved it.

More than six million women
worked in the war industries,
about one for every Jew
murdered by the Nazis.
We made over three hundred thousand airplanes,
more than a hundred thousand tanks.

I loved it so much,
I stayed on ten more years after the war ended,
until I was forced into retirement.
My single regret?
We never used any of the weapons
to go after the Bolsheviks.

Retirement

After I was forced to retire from factory work
because of my "age" (I wasn't even 60),
having already re-located from Miami to San Pedro,
I lived in Los Angeles on my Social Security benefits,
teaching Russian, and babysitting.

Sometimes I'd be in the newspapers,
like when I saw Betty Ford in my dreams,
or the time I supported Anna Anderson's claim
she was the Grand Duchess Anastasia.
I later recanted, but for a minute
I truly believed the old imposter.

Well, I was an old woman then, too,
living alone in Silverlake, the LA neighborhood
where all the Russian émigrés lived,
with my two little dogs,
Youssou and Pov, named for Felix Yusupov,
one of my father's assassins.

But I ended up a lot better than my own mother,
Praskovya, who was kicked out of the home
in Pokrovskoe where she and Papa
had raised a family in their fashion.
For the next ten years Mama and my brother Dmitry
lived in a hovel on the edge of the village
until 1930 when the Soviets decided they were kulaks,
class enemies of the state,

banished them to work on constructing a cannery
on the Ob River in remote Siberia,
where they died several years later,
dysentery and heart failure.

SASHA

Operation Former People

It was right around the time we went to New York
I started hearing the rumors,
somebody shot Sergei Kirov, Leningrad's
Communist party secretary, in the head.
Some people said Stalin was behind it,
ridding himself of a potential rival,
but within two months, the NKVD
set about ridding the city
of every remaining former person –
not just nobles, tsarist military and police officers, Orthodox
clergymen,
but "the counter-revolutionary reserve" as well –
their children and grandchildren:
a campaign called Operation Former People,
so-called after Maxim Gorky's 1897 story,
"Byvshie lyudi," translated in English as
"Creatures that Once Were Men." *Former People:*
over eleven thousand arrested or deported within a month,
"age-old exploiters and bloodsuckers," "tsarist scum,"
"parasites,"
as the local press called them – *Leningradkaia Pravda,*
copies of which had somehow come to Baltimore.

And oh, how relieved I felt,
slipping into bed with Riva,
our American children nearby,
safe to the extent
Jews are ever safe in this world.

Yezhovshchina

It would go on for more than a decade,
the Great Terror, but it was
the Moscow show trials of 1937 and 1938
that snagged our imagination, the rumors
filling us with jaw-dropping horror;
Nikolai Yezhov, the ceremonial ringmaster,
organizing the three tribunals,
culminating in the trial of the
"Anti-Soviet Block of Rightists and Trotskyites."

The outcome? Stalin's former ally, Bukharin,
once editor of the party newspaper, *Pravda,*
after the October Revolution, shot along with
Genrikh Yagoda, head of the NKVD;
Yagoda'd been replaced by Yezhov.

And Yezhov? Pursued the great terror with great zeal,
over three quarters of a million people arrested,
half of them executed; so enthusiastic, in fact,
party leadership in Moscow started talking about "excesses."
So Stalin made Yezhov the scapegoat for his terror campaign,
forced him to retire, then had him shot
in an execution chamber built to Yezhov's own design in
Moscow.

Stalin replaced him with the Georgian party boss,
Lavrenty Beria, who'd similarly be shot
after Stalin died, the Politburo squabbling for control,
Khrushchev coming out on top – for a time.

What a relief to live
in a country where politics
was all about elections.

Lev

When I read about Trotsky's assassination,
Mexico City, August, 1940,
a little more than a year before
the Japanese bombed Pearl Harbor,
my Hermie and Reuben destined for the draft –
and who knows? Maybe Sammy, too,
if the war lasted long enough –
I remembered my uncle, murdered in Kiev.
Both named Lev.

Trotsky changed his name to hide his Jewishness –
Lev Bronstein his birth name –
but also because the Russian government
wanted him for his revolutionary activities.
He'd organized workers as early as the 1890's,
jailed, exiled to Siberia, spent years in Europe
before joining the Bolsheviks,
Lenin's righthand man.
Isolated by Stalin, he was murdered with an ice axe.

But a Jew, in some ways
as much a victim as my uncle,
beaten by the peasant mob before my eyes
that October afternoon when I was ten,
a fit of self-righteous bloodlust –

all Russia's problems, they declared,
justifying their brutality,
stemming from the machinations
of Jews and Socialists.

Night of the Murdered Poets

The night of my first grandchild's birth,
Reuben and Leah's son Lev,
named in honor of my uncle,
slain in the Kiev pogrom forty-seven years before,
I'd later learn also marked
what we called in Yiddish
Harugey malkus funem Ratnfarband –
Soviet Union Martyrs,
what the Russians referred to as
the Jewish Anti-Fascists Committee Affair –
Delo Yevreyskogo antifashistskogo komiteta,
the night the NKVD murdered
thirteen Soviet Jews in Moscow's Lubyanka Prison,
on dummy charges of treason and espionage,
"counterrevolutionary crimes" with the intent
to "topple, undermine and weaken the Soviet Union,"
including an attempt to establish Crimea as the new Jewish
homeland.

After years of interrogations beatings, torture –
they'd been arrested in 1948 and 1949 –
the trial took place the summer of 1952
before a three-judge military tribunal,
the defendants including Yiddish poets, novelists, editors,
the actual executions August 12.

But nobody knew for years,
nothing in the newspapers;
not until 1955,
long after Stalin's death,
the proceedings reexamined,
the Soviet court determining
"no substance to the charges," the case closed.

That was November 22,
the day Frieda's twins were born,
Sarah and Rebecca.

The Doctors' Plot

Sometime later in the 1950's
when the new Soviet leader, Khrushchev,
gave his speech "On the Cult of Personality and Its
Consequences"
to the Congress of the Communist Party
we learned about the Doctors' Plot,
by rumor and report and hearsay,
terrifying as a wicked fairy tale:
Stalin's anti-Semitic campaign to rid Russia of Jews,
dummied reports of a conspiracy of Jewish doctors,
led by Yakov Etinger, to kill the Soviet leadership,
about the same time as the Night of the Murdered Poets.
Etinger died in prison, after being tortured.

Khrushchev claimed Stalin's plan was a show trial,
to launch a Communist Party purge,
deport Soviet Jews to Siberian labor camps,
an ambitious program of Jewish genocide;
the Jewish doctors on trial
would be executed in Red Square.
Nikolai Bulgarin claimed Stalin asked him to prepare
railroad cars for the mass deportation of Jews to Siberia –
"pure-blooded Jews" first, then the half-breeds,
the *polukrovki*.

And pogroms! Khrushchev claimed Stalin planned
to incite antisemitism in Ukraine.
"The good workers of the factory should be given clubs,"

Stalin declared, "so they can beat the hell out of those Jews."

And then Stalin died, and all the charges dropped,
the Doctors' plot found to be fabricated,
the doctors exonerated.

In America some of us still feared
there would come a knock on the door one night.
Was an ocean enough to protect us?

Clothes Make the Woman

"Anastasia screamed in vain." – *"Sympathy for the Devil"*

Forty years earlier I'd seen the silent film,
Eve Southern as the teenaged princess,
Walter Pidgeon the Russian revolutionary
who rescues her from execution.

Rumors of her escape multiplied like all urban legends,
fueled by the fact the mass grave near Yekaterinburg
embraced only the bodies of Nicholas, Alexandra,
the other three daughters.

People reported seeing Anastasia at railway stations.
Maria Rasputin's husband, Boris Soloviev,
defrauded wealthy families, getting money
to help the princess escape to China,
even persuaded a young woman
to masquerade as the Tsar's youngest daughter.

Then, in 1968, Maria Rasputin authenticated the claims
of the latest imposter, Anna Anderson,
Only three years older than the princess,
Maria met Anna and after several hours,
declared Anna the real Anastasia.
Anna'd been fighting legal battles since 1938,
officially filed in the German courts.

Later, Maria took back the claim
when Anderson refused
to dine with her in Los Angeles
under the name of Anastasia Romanov –
though I think she realized her mistake.

Otkaznik

After the Six-Day War in 1967,
Riva's nephew Khaim, a physician in Novosibirsk,
applied for an exit visa to make aliyah to Israel,
sick of the antisemitism, to join his brother's family.
His application languished for years in the MVD.
The authorities claimed he had access
to information vital to Soviet national security,
though for the life of him, he didn't know what.

Khaim participated in a demonstration in Moscow,
with a dozen other refuseniks,
carrying a banner that read,
"Let us go to our families in Israel."
The authorities arrested him in Dzershinsky Square
on charges of "hooliganism,"
in violation of an article in the Penal Code.

The only employer in the Soviet Union,
the government punished him by firing him
for daring to apply for the visa.
Accused then of social parasitism,
he was sent to Arkhangelsk Oblast,
in the frozen north, where he died.

The old joke applied to Khaim:
The KGB demands to know why
he's applied for a visa.

"Here in Russia you don't get enough food?"

"I can't complain."

"You don't have a job?"

"I can't complain."

"So why do you want to move to Israel?"

"Because there I *can* complain...."

MARIA

The Legend

I never actually saw it,
so I don't know –
Papa always modest around Varvara and me.
But I always suspected
it was like the tale of the fisherman's catch
that keeps growing in the re-telling,
though who knows?

Of course, I heard all the bawdy poems,
saw the smutty graffiti.
The walls of Ipatiev House –
the House of Special Purpose –
where the Romanov family was executed,
covered with crude drawings,
lurid as American comic books,
Papa and Alexandra in lewd poses
while Nicholas looked on, drinking –
Papa's manhood depicted big as a whale –
over some doggerel about "Grishka and Sashova."

Of all the heartbreaking incidents
in that wild, chaotic time,
it's the image of Nicholas and Alexandra,
followed by Olga, Tatiana, Maria, Anastasia and Alexei,
led by the guards at the House of Special Purpose

down those twenty-three wooden steps,
past the offensive, grotesque pornography,
into the basement that July day in 1918,
that really brings tears to my eyes.

Rasputin's Eyes

I inherited Papa's eyes.
Ringling Brothers claimed
it's what made the animals obey me,
though I never believed
that rubbish for a moment.

Still, Yelena Dzhanumova,
one of Papa's many female admirers,
swore his gaze was so intense
it could make a woman shake
and fall into hysterics.

My husband Boris' father,
Nikolai Solovyov, told the press,
"The charm of this man lies in his eyes.
There's something in them
that draws you in and forces you
to submit to his will."

"His eyes pierced you liked needles,"
Lydia Bazilevskaya, a wealthy divorcée exclaimed,
while that prig Alexander Prugavin described them as
"the green rapacious fires of a voluptuary."

"While that gaze held me," Meriel Buchanan,
daughter of the British ambassador declared,
"I was possessed
by a sensation of helplessness so intense."

Who knows? His eyes,
like reassuring beacons in the night,
always told me I was safe,
Papa loved me.

SASHA

Obituary

I read the news that day, oh boy,
to quote that song my grandson Lev,
thoroughly American, not a trace
of the Pale, kept raving about a decade ago –
the words just as devastating:
Maria Rasputin Soloviev Bern,
dancer, circus performer,
co-author with Pattie Barham of
Rasputin: The Man Behind the Myth,
found dead in her home in Silverlake,
a Los Angeles suburb,
the walls of her home
covered with pictures of her father,
the Russian aristocracy.
Earlier she'd called a neighbor –
she'd been having trouble breathing.

I remembered seeing her for the first time
all those years ago, in St. Petersburg,
with her father's secretary, Aaron Simanovich,
another Jew, and only now
did the force of my attraction, then,
hit me like a fist.
Yes, all this time,

I'd been secretly in love with Maria –
at 82, over fifty years married,
children and grandchildren abundant as fruit,
reduced to a lovesick teenage boy,
Lev and I having more in common
than I'd usually admit.

Hitler Is Alive in Argentina

I bought the book Maria wrote
with somebody named Pattie Barham,
published around the time she died in 1977.
She made her father out to be a saint,
as any loving daughter might do,
but the lurid detail that stood out for me,
a meeting described in Barham's Afterword.

Her claim to fame being the first
female war correspondent in Korea,
Barham wrote about a secret meeting in Paris
where she'd gone in 1968 to meet Maria
and her daughter Tatiana.
A White Russian peasant named Georges
called Pattie at her hotel on the Rue St. Honoré,
took her to meet his grandmother,
who'd been a maid at the Hotel Europe in Saint Petersburg,
where she'd had an affair with Rasputin.
In a polished wooden box with an inlaid silver crest
the old woman had what looked like
"a blackened, overripe banana about a foot long,"
displayed in a velvet cloth.

The old woman told Barham
one of the servants in Rasputin's assassin's house,
married to her sister,
retrieved the severed penis for her.
The grandmother'd had sex with Rasputin
to purge her of her sins: a holy act.

Reading this, I thought of the fantastic stories
I read in the grocery store tabloids,
Outer-space aliens, Bigfoot, and the like.

Catastroika

The wordplay in the press on Perestroika,
Gorbachev's program of economic reforms –
Catastrophe. Me? I was comfortable
after a lifetime in the furniture business in Baltimore,
but Russia was still alive in my dreams
more than sixty years since I got out.

It was glasnost that gave me heart – "openness."
On the fiftieth anniversary of Babi Yar,
the 1941 pogrom in Kiev,
thirty thousand Jews slaughtered,
Gorbachev acknowledged decades of anti-Semitic
discrimination;
he'd granted Jews – many refuseniks – the right to emigrate,
but he regretted the departure of so many talented citizens:
half a million gone to Israel,
a quarter million to the United States and elsewhere.

But if life's improved for Jews under Gorbachev,
the general economic situation's deteriorated,
Jewish leaders fearing Jews will be blamed,
the usual scapegoats.

Rasputin Rehabilitated

And Maria's father?
Since the collapse of the Soviet Union,
his reputation seems to have improved.

The Communists hated holy men anyway,
let alone a favorite of the tsar and his wife.
They made Rasputin out to be the devil incarnate,
spreading rumors about his immoral behavior,
undermining the legitimacy of the throne,
an attempt to wipe out Russian Orthodoxy.

But now the priests are back!
They're trying to confer sainthood on Rasputin!
In fact, one branch of the church already has –
the Russian True Orthodox Church.

I am so relieved we Jews
do not worry about sainthood,
elevating humans to godlike status.
We have enough trouble keeping track
of our martyrs.

Saint Petersburg

Saint Petersburg: a monument to himself,
Peter the Great planned and constructed it 1703,
a port city on the Baltic,
patterned on a dream
of the great cities of Europe he'd visited
in his youth, particularly Amsterdam.

During the war with Germany,
the government wanted something
more "Russian-sounding,"
so they called the city Petrograd in 1914.

Ten years later, a monument to Lenin.
The Bolsheviks toppled the monarchy in 1917,
created the Soviet Union in 1922,
and when Lenin died in 1924,
the city took his name. Leningrad.

Me, I called it Petrograd all along,
after I left Russia in 1919,
settling in the United States, in Baltimore,
and now, when I've turned 96 – *96!* –
they've changed the name back to Saint Petersburg.

The diehard Bolsheviks see this
as a slap in the face to Lenin,
but others see it as a way past
the grim Communist era,

as if you can erase History.
But fifty-five percent of the citizens
voted for the name change –
just as all Russia voted for Yeltsin.
Doesn't mean much to me.
I've got a plot in the Chizuk Amuno cemetery
on Rogers Ave., next to my Riva,
whom I expect to be lying
next to again, soon.

Glossary

Narodnaya Volya – The People's Will, a 19th-century revolutionary political organization in the Russian Empire

Milochka – Dear

Strannik – A religious pilgrim in Russia

Yezhovshchina – The great purge, after Nikolai Yezhov, the head of the Soviet secret police, the NKVD

Otkaznik – Refusenik

Proizvol – Arbitrary will, power abuse, lawlessness

Byvshie lyudi – former people (Gorky)

Acknowledgements

Bindweed – "Sightseeing in Saint Petersburg"

Former People – "Byvshie lyudi," "Operation Former People," "*Yezhovshchina*"

Harbinger Asylum – "Harry Houdini Gets out of Russia

Alive," "Maria Rasputin, Lion Tamer," "Maria Rasputin Leaves Siberia," "Prophecy"

I would also like to thank Kevin Atticks, Annabelle Finagin and all of the Apprentice House staff for making this book possible.

Biographical Note

Charles Rammelkamp received an MA in English Literature from Boston University and an MA in Publication Design with a Specialization in Creative Writing from the University of Baltimore. He has published a novel, *The Secretkeepers* (Red Hen Press), two collections of short fiction, *A Better Tomorrow* (PublishAmerica) and *Castleman in the Academy* (March Street Press), and four previous collections of poetry, *The Book of Life* (March Street Press), *Fusen Bakudan* (Time Being Books), and two previous titles from Apprentice House, *Mata Hari: Eye of the Day* and *American Zeitgeist*. Two recent poetry chapbooks are also available: *Jack Tar's Lady Parts* (Main Street Rag Press) and *Me and Sal Paradise* (FutureCycle Press).

Rammelkamp worked as a technical writer for various companies and organizations throughout his career, including the Social Security Administration, from which he retired in 2014. He edited *The Potomac: A Journal of Politics and Poetry* for ten years and is currently Prose Editor for BrickHouse Books in Baltimore and Reviews Editor for The *Adirondack Review*. He lives in Baltimore with his wife, Abby, to whom he's been married for about a million years. They have two daughters and two grandchildren.

Apprentice
House Press
Loyola University Maryland

Apprentice House is the country's only campus-based, student-staffed book publishing company. Directed by professors and industry professionals, it is a nonprofit activity of the Communication Department at Loyola University Maryland.

Using state-of-the-art technology and an experiential learning model of education, Apprentice House publishes books in untraditional ways. This dual responsibility as publishers and educators creates an unprecedented collaborative environment among faculty and students, while teaching tomorrow's editors, designers, and marketers.

Outside of class, progress on book projects is carried forth by the AH Book Publishing Club, a co-curricular campus organization supported by Loyola University Maryland's Office of Student Activities.

Eclectic and provocative, Apprentice House titles intend to entertain as well as spark dialogue on a variety of topics. Financial contributions to sustain the press's work are welcomed. Contributions are tax deductible to the fullest extent allowed by the IRS.

To learn more about Apprentice House books or to obtain submission guidelines, please visit www.apprenticehouse.com.

Apprentice House
Communication Department
Loyola University Maryland
4501 N. Charles Street
Baltimore, MD 21210
Ph: 410-617-5265 • Fax: 410-617-2198
info@apprenticehouse.com • www.apprenticehouse.com